D1476415

PERFORMANCE ONE
Monologues for Women

PERFORMANCE ONE

by

William-Alan Landes

WILTSHIRE LIBRARY & MUSEUM SERVICE

THE LIBRARY
WITHDRAWN
SWINDON

PLAYERS PRESS
Studio City, California
U.S.A.

A.C.T.
AUSTRALIA

Essex
UNITED KINGDOM

20 00004387

PERFORMANCE ONE

© Copyright, 1991, by William-Alan Landes
© Copyright, 1991, PHOTOS, William-Alan Landes
ISBN 0-88734-122-5
Library of Congress Catalog Number: 91-52959

All rights reserved; no part of this publication may be reproduced, stored in a retrieval system, or transmitted in any form or by any means, electronic, mechanical, photocopying, recording, or otherwise, without the prior permission of the Publishers.

PLAYERS PRESS, Inc.
P.O. Box 1132
Studio City, CA 91614-0132, U.S.A.

812.046

Library of Congress Cataloging-in-Publication Data

Landes, William-Alan.
    Performance one : monologues for women / by
William-Alan Landes.
        p.   cm.
    ISBN 0-88734-122-5 (pbk.) : $15.95
    1.Monologues. 2. Acting--Auditions. 3. Women--Drama.
I. Title.
PN2080.L29 1991
808.82'45'082--dc20   91-52959
                                                              CIP

Printed in U.S.A.
Simultaneously Published in U.S.A., U.K. and Australia

Dedicated
to
Sharon Gorrell Hoffman

My dearest friend and love of over twenty-one years,
who was the inspiration and is the embodiment of
many of my characters herein.

Love always,
William

PREFACE

The entire auditioning system is an unnatural act. We as performers are stripped of all the trappings and personalization that make it possible to generate the emotion of a performance, thrown on a bare platform, with harsh or insufficient light and ordered -- *ACT*. But we survive and many thrive, and we must, if we are to fulfill our need or desire to be in front of an audience. Careful selection of material will help reclothe and arm you against the unnaturalness of this system.

Searching for an audition monologue seems like an endless quest. It is a chore that cannot be avoided and should not be taken lightly. The material you choose to present may determine whether you get hired, which part you do get or if you are to be in the show at all.

Too often, in auditions, we see the same choices of monologues. This overuse of material just emphasizes a lack of acting craft; the selection of your material is as important, if not more important, than the presentation. If my writing, here, accomplishes nothing else but to impress that you should take the extra time necessary to find those special words, that make your choice of monologues stand out, then I will have succeeded.

I have spent a large percent of my career on both sides of the theatrical fence - Acting/Casting. The most difficult fact and an item frequently discussed is "How many times will we see the same monologue during this series of auditions?" The answer is always the same - "Too many times."

I remember once having an actress, at a comedy workshop at Merrick Studios, play devil's advocate. She took the opposite point of view and tried to defend the merits of using the well-known monologues. "You have a chance to display your ability in a known piece." "The Audition Board has a basis of comparison." "It shows the performer is willing to tackle the great roles." Joe E. Ross and Scatman Cruthers, studio guests, quickly responded: Joe E. said, "It doesn't work that way. It would be like trying to use the same old joke that everyone knows, you have no punch line." Scatman said, "You have to stand out, be different, be remembered." Joe E. did his, "ooh ohh" and the point was well taken. Avoid the familiar and search for the special piece that will showcase you. If you want to study a great monologue - do it on your own or in a workshop, not at an audition.

Even in presenting the Classics, selecting those "famous monologues" for an audition is usually the best way to lose the part. There is a wide and varied range of Classic monologues. Everyone should not be Hamlet.

At the Group, we were casting a summer series of Shakespeare. We had 82 male auditions, Hamlet's "To be or not to be..." speech was presented 22 times. We also had 94 female auditions: 11 Lady Macbeth, washing blood; 14 Juliet, on the balcony; and 10 Shrewish Kates. There also were some very interesting selections, these, unfortunately, were in the minority. As a point of reference, most of the performers with the "interesting selections" were on the call back list.

There is only one audition where you *must* present that overused monologue; that is when you are assigned that particular piece. But, please, do it with style - your style.

The performer has a definite advantage with a less familiar cutting. Good or Bad, you are judged on your presentation. The observers not only watch the performance but want to listen and hear the words. You as the performer receive more of the observers' attention. They want to find out what will happen and how you will make it happen because they may not know. They also will not be running the lines in their heads, because they know them better than the person auditioning. Several times I've noticed, at Castings, one of my colleagues shaking his head - later to hear, "It would be nice if that performer could have come close to the words the author wrote." Obviously that performer was not on the call back list.

There are many available cuttings that have the power of emotion and srength of word that are not repeatedly over-used. It is essential that you take the time to locate, rehearse and personalize each monologue. It is also critical that you constantly update and expand your audition repertoire.

Although selecting monologue material is crucial, it is only part of the audition process. You must also develop your own style, understand yourself as a performer, highlight your special attributes, open your emotions so you can express them freely, and develop a comfortable manner and grace to bring each character and yourself before an audience; even if the audience is an auditor of one.

It is an enormous task that many performers, with a good deal of painstaking hard work, accomplish and even make look easy; but that is what acting, *doing*, is all about.

Eventually you will collect and develop a repertoire of monologues that are both comfortable and work well for you at auditions. If you are to succeed, you will also develop that sense of who you are and what you have to offer to an audience.

This book, and the series PERFORMANCE WORKSHOP, should help fill some of the needs for available material and direction on how to use the material.

William-Alan Landes

Amy Ardavany

CONTENTS

INTRODUCTION

In this book the actress and the director, as well as the drama student can find a wide range of compelling monologues for auditions and practice. The material represents a variety of modern characters that should offer challenging roles for the professional as well as the student.

This selection of monologues was specifically cut so that minimal production requirements - costumes, scenery, props, lights, etc. - are needed. Several of the monologues require no trappings at all, showcasing only the abilities of actress and director.

The variety of character types and dimension within each character can help the actress demonstrate her range and depth of ability. The student can use this same variety to develop and expand abilities, learning about the process of character study and individual presentation. Analyzing the characters and developing the needed techniques to understand and relate the scripted words to the performance can expand insights into these characters as well as carry over into future acting roles.

Brief introductions to each monologue give general background that may help understand the characters. Each monologue was also chosen so that very little background information is necessary; in this way the selections will stand by themselves on the moment-by-moment performance of the actress and the conflicts within the written work.

Any good director will tell you that there can be numerous interpretations for each role. There is, of course, no *right* way to play a role; how you approach a monologue depends largely on the analysis of the character and the circumstances. Part of the theatrical magic is that no actor or director will interpret a dramatic piece quite the same as another actor or director. Each person will bring something different and special to their interpretation.

Both director and actress need to carefully analyze the monologue. Each should set and determine their overall conception and define the characterization then blend the concept to follow a single course. Through the rehearsal process, the actress must detail specifics of character and action polishing the monologue for performance.

Understanding and adhering to the positions of director and performer will usually improve the final presentation and make the rehearsal period more productive and harmonious.

The director should prepare the overall interpretation for the monologue and the overall character analysis in relation to the planned presentation. For young directors, and especially performers trying to direct themselves, I always advise that you work out as much directorial detail for your performer and relate your overall approach to the specifics you want your characterization and action to take. Do not leave large gaps to be worked out later. Even outlines for blocking and movement should be pre-prepared; they can, and usually are, modified during rehearsal as you interact with your performer. The preparation will give you an air of confidence and, for these monologues, a basis to grow from.

The actress has an obligation of preparing the character and developing a complete interpretation of how the character fits into the action. The specific subtleties of characterization that personalize a performance are usually the performer's domain; each needs the director's approval so that the final performance creates a uniform presentation of character, combining the overall director's concept with the specifically detailed performer's interpretation, blending harmoniously with the other characters.

It is important that both performer and director be aware that, even in a monologue, you may need to blend the single on-stage entity with one or more offstage or unseen presences. The performer may speak or need to react to an

2

offstage character. An unseen presence, whether real or imaginary may plague the onstage performer.

Discussions of interpretations, characterizations, blocking, etc. will stimulate the creative process. It is the director's responsibility for the total production, even in a monologue. It is the performer's job to unite the written words with the inner emotions in such a way that the script breathes life, a moment at a time. The director will sketch the picture but the performer must fill in the detail and color within the director's lines.

For the following monologues I recommend the major concentration of time being spent on rehearsal and character analysis. Textual research should not be necessary, because as previously stated, these cuttings were selected to eliminate the need to study the entire play. They were chosen to give powerful scripts for short presentations.

The brief introductions give general information about the play, monologue and characters. The cuttings, themselves, will then supply the necessary information to establish a character base. From this base, director and actress should build the final characterization. It is the actress' individual character and background that should be added. Director and Actress should use as much of the actress' personal life to quickly build the needed subtext. Remember to feel the words and emotions evoked by the monologue, so as to free the personal inner being. Do not trap the performance in too much intellectualization; *acting is doing*, and the character portrayed must live.

Because I feel that researching the full play is unnecessary and may inhibit the creative process in preparing these particular monologues, does not mean that each monologue is set in stone and cannot vary. The opposite is true. The material is extremely flexible and unlimited interpretations are available to the creative mind.

Now, select and prepare your monologue; choose the material that *suits you* and that you can present in a believable manner.

PREPARATION

The following is a basic analysis that may be used to assist in the preparation of these monologues. It is only meant as a guide and there are many equally fine ways to approach the material.

DIRECTOR:

The director should prepare his overall approach and set the mood or atmosphere. The mood or atmosphere, whether comic, tragic, inspirational, nostalgic, or a combination of these must be maintained to produce the desired effect. Costume, Scenery and Props should, for an audition, be minimal. Movement, action and performance are primary in monologue presentation.

Next the director develops his character approach. How does each character fit into the overall concept of the monologue? Why are they included? How does each character advance the plot? These questions and more form the basis of the prepatory outline determining the overall approach the director will take to develop the basic character traits and how the different characters relate to each other. As above, I mentioned "each character", beware not to omit any offstage characters or any needed onstage presense. Building on this overall character approach, the director will then determine how the characters advance the theme and represent the basic qualities needed or wanted, and how these needs or wants come into conflict, on stage, with the monologue's action.

Once the overall directorial approach has been determined the director must bring this approach to bear on the individual and specific elements of character and production. Blocking the performer for the monologue, should follow. Remember to always keep a detailed prompt book.

The inter-relationship of director, performer and stage space dominate the rehearsal. Often what looks good on paper or in the mind of the director or peformer will not always look good or even work with and for the performer on stage. Blocking is often changed throughout the rehearsal period.

The elements of a rehearsal, vary according to the director, but generally follow a pattern from blocking, to character and line study, to final polish and lastly the technical production elements. For a monologue character; blocking, line and polish should be the main elements.

PERFORMER (ACTRESS):

The performer may prepare an outline analysis, much like the director or may use a freer approach and try to emotionalize the work. Personally, I prefer a combination of the two which allows the overall approach more flexibility so that it may comfortably blend with the director's approach, the author's words and the emotion and senses of the performer. The specific and personal detail are where the performer should place the most emphasis.

As a guide for starting with this material I suggest that you read a monologue and allow yourself to flow with the words and feel the emotions. Let your own feelings fill the void between words and character. Pour your heart, soul and mind into the emotional outcry of tears, anger, anguish, pain, etc., try to remember as much of why this happened so you can use it again. Let the words touch you and if they rattle free an emotional expression save it and savour its useage.

Next, analyze the material. Ask yourself -- how would I react to these words and situations? What would I do in this circumstance? Then do what you say you would do with the words and read it again. Put down the author's words. Reach out, let yourself free, and expand the feelings that could be available for the situation.

Once you are comfortable with the material, from your readings and improvisations, then start your written analysis. Remember, you need and want to find answers for those questions that will help you evoke the feelings you felt as you read the monologue. You may also want to find answers for questions that developed through your improvisation of the material.

Personalization analysis is the next important element. What do I have in common with this character? What situations, from my life, could cause me to feel or say the words within the monologue? How did I feel when those situations occurred? Now moving towards the specific and emphasizing color and tone: How do I feel now, because of those specific situations? What feelings do the words evoke as I read or say them? Why do the words make me feel this way? What images are brought to mind? How can I recreate these images each time I present the words?

These questions are but a few that need and will be asked. Once you or the director begin the process more and more questions will be added. This is where most of the study and rehearsal time for these monologues should be concentrated. There is no particular place or order that is best in analyzing a character.

HYPHENATE (PERFORMER/DIRECTOR):

The most difficult concern most performers can have should be whether or not they must undertake the directorial task themselves. Some will do a marvelous job of performer/director but most will not. Whenever possible the performer should seek out a director. The collaborative process usually improves the final performance. If a director is not available or you just want to stick your head in the lion's mouth, consider finding a director just to critique before you finalize your performance. This second sight may help polish or save your presentation.

ANALYSIS

GENERAL (ACTRESS/DIRECTOR):

1. What are the most important lines and where are the high points?

   Discovering or selecting this can help plan the director's blocking and emphasize the specific ideas and main speeches.

2. How do the characters interact? What relationship exists between them? What emotional ties do they have?

3. What are the circumstances of time and place? Where is the action taking place?

DIRECTOR:

1. What are the basic traits and goals of each character? Do they like or dislike each other? What character conflicts exist? Who is the monologue's most important character? Why? How can this importance be emphasized? What stereotypes exist in each character? Should they be emphasized? What is unique about each character? What is ordinary?

2. Which lines of dialogue are important in establishing character? In advancing plot? How can they be emphasized? Should they be underplayed or pointed up to the audience?

3. What is the subject matter of the monologue? Why is it important? Why would an audience want to see this monologue? How can I maintain the interest for the audience? Heighten their interest?

4. What is the mood or atmosphere? What production technical elements (set, costume, lights, etc.) best portray this? How can I eliminate the production elements and still maintain the atmosphere? Heighten the mood?

5. What are my space confines? How can I expand the space? Shrink the space? Concentrate attention on a specific space?

6. What will my performer bring to this character? How can I incorporate, evaluate, eliminate my ideas, her ideas?

ACTRESS:

1. What is the background of my character? Education? Family? Environment? What significant incidents have shaped my character? Which are the most important?

2. What are the interests and goals of my character? Work? Hobbies? Play? Love? Hate? How does my character spend free time?

3. What type of possessions does my character have? Enjoy? Want? How would my character furnish a home? An office? Why?

4. How does my character feel about the other characters? About the world in general? In specific? About self?

5. What specific traits are evident about my character? Happy or unhappy? What impresses or fails to impress others about my character? What are the most important aspects of personality? My personality?

6. Does my character have friends? Do I want them? Need them? Why?

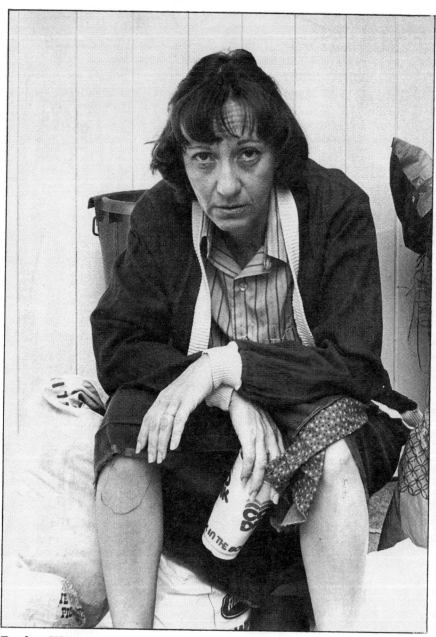

Roslyn Witt

PART I

This section consists of monologues cut from award winning, critically acclaimed, and/or successfully produced productions of Mr. Landes' plays.

MISPLACED LOVE

The premier production was in 1971 as an evening of one acts at the Actor's Quest Theatre in Hollywood. The play was submitted at the urging of Leonard Spieglegas, author of MAJORITY OF ONE who was the instructor for a writing seminar at the University of Southern California. The play was selected as the first place Winner.

The story centers around Margaret and Joseph Carter. It deals with the disintegration of their marriage from Margaret's misconception of the feminist movement of the 60's and the emergence of women as stronger, more dominant figures within television situations.

Margaret and Joe are truly in love with each other. They have been in love since High School. Joe doesn't want to deal with the *new* person -- he *cannot* understand her *changes* but he is willing to do anything to make her happy. There is nothing he can do.

Margaret's crisis is that she now wants to reevaluate her life; turn back the clock and relive her opportunities. She is looking for something that she really doesn't want to find -- *herself as a new woman.*

If this cloud, that has engulfed her, would pass, she could see that she is happy with her position as wife. For the moment, she can see nothing but her misconception of the New Woman. She feels she cannot be content as just Joe's wife.

The action takes place in the living room of the Carter home of fifteen years. Margaret is neatly but plainly dressed. Her choice of fashion and hair style place her slightly older than her years.

The characteristic that permeates everything about this woman is her genuine human warmth. It is this warmth and her love for Joe that is the counterpoint of her conflict.

MARGARET. *(Pacing, frustrated. She unleashes her fury.)* Don't you understand? I'm fed up! No, I'm not talking housework. I'm telling you about my life. Living, day to day. US!

(She nervously plays with her wedding ring, moving it up and down, over the knuckle.)

I don't care if I sound like the women on television. *(She drops the ring and picks it up.)* This is supposed to be...a partnership. *(She stares at the ring as she slides it back on her finger.)* You and I...Two people working together for the same goals; both receiving the benefits...I don't seem to be getting anything and you're getting everything. Something is wrong!

(She looks up as he tries to respond.)

No. I have no objection to your being happy, but not at my expense. I think I do enough to make you happy. What do you do to make me happy?

(Again he tries to respond.)

That doesn't work anymore!

(She watches his defeat...)

I'll tell you where it's all going. Nowhere! It's been going nowhere for a long time. I keep deluding myself that we'll work it out; but we don't. It's time for a change. We're due for a change. Hopefully for the better.

(She crosses right, stops, turns back to answer him.)

I don't call it selfish. But, if finally taking care of myself is selfish then you're right; I may be selfish. I may have always been selfish. Aren't we all? You certainly are!

(Her words echo feminism but from her they seem out of place.)

You know, I don't think I have ever been an understanding woman. I think I've tried. I know I've done everything possible...everything I could do...to understand you and your needs. Now, as far as I'm concerned, it is your responsibility to make and keep me happy. I want you to make me happy! *(There is a moment as she reflects on her words.)*

(She laughs lightly.) That was a rather foolish statement. *(Realizing what may have taken place.)* I summed it up nicely. It's not you. *(Choking on her words.)* It's me. It seems you were right.

(She understands.)

What do I...What do we do now?

(There is a moment of painful silence.)

If you don't know...I surely don't. I cannot go on the way it is. Not because of you...because of me.

(She finds some comfort in her understanding.)

Everything seems suddenly clear. I've been picking a fight with you every time I didn't get what I felt I should have. I've kept it inside...you couldn't even know what I wanted, but I blamed you for not giving it to me. Maybe, I've been unreasonable?

(Hurting.) I started this...argument...with my mind set on a divorce...now...all I want is for you...*(She feels hopelessly alone.)* Please, hold me. *(She crosses her arms in front, holding herself...waiting...)*

I'm sorry...so very sorry.

New White

This monologue was cut from a skit which was part of a Musical Review, WEDDING WHITE, produced off Broadway by Theatre Unique.

Jan is a late bloomer. She's made a place for herself as a book buyer and has done very well, in business. Her love life has been a terrible disappointment and Jan desperately wants a change.

David Billings, a salesman, has swept her off her feet, at least that's what David believes. In actuality, Jan's mom has coached her every step of the way and to Jan's surprise, Mom has been right.

As they approach the big day, Jan decided to handle one small problem without Mom's help.

The action takes place in Jan's apartment. In the production Jan was dressed in her wedding gown -- but it is not necessary.

Jan's conflict is that she's terribly disappointed about cancelling the wedding but relieved about not having to marry David.

JAN. *(Shakes her head in disbelief.)* Three days before the wedding. I thought everything was perfect. We're in love. *(She hesitates.)* He loved me...no...I was...I am in love with him. I don't know what I'm going

to do. We have already had the wedding rehearsal.
Everyone knows.

At first he didn't want to get married. You know how
men talk. My mom was wonderful; she really knew what
to do. I never expected her to be the one to tell me to go to bed
with a man before I was married.

"Hook him with good food." Silly but true. "The way to a
man's heart" and all that...Mom was a good teacher. I
like to cook. She really threw me when she asked "Have
you been to bed with him?" *(Speaking to her mother.)* No,
Mom! I'm really saving it for a wedding night. "I think
that's nice, but at your age a bit impractical. He's not
going to propose under those terms." She was right. Just
enough...and I got a ring and a proposal.

(Coming down.)

Tomorrow's the big day. But of course it's not, now. I
can't believe us. He wouldn't give an inch. *(Ashamed.)*
Neither would I. In two days everything seems to have
changed. Can love be that fleeting?

It seems...I...I thought I could sway him. I asked...It
went well at first. Yesterday I felt he was trying. Then,
today, he exploded. "You're unreasonable..." I tried to
explain. I shouldn't have had to. He should have
understood. He didn't. I can still hear the door slam.

(She stands silently, watching.)

Now, I've got to tell everyone. How am I going to do
it?...and Dad...He's going to be mad. *(She smiles.)* No!
He'll understand; if anyone understands. He won't like
spending all that money but he'll understand. He's a
funny man. *(Lovingly.)* My dad! We're all afraid of his
temper, but he's always there when you need him.

(She looks at herself in the mirror.)

Is it really going to end like this? A few hours ago...then he was going to think about it. Now it's over. *(Looking off.)* Is it really over? *(She has no answer.)*

I handled it right. I didn't demand. I asked. *(Realizing.)* If I handled it right it wouldn't be over.

(She picks up her veil.)

It smells awful! His clothes...everything...He could have tried. *(Smelling herself.)* I'm beginning to reek of it.

Maybe it just wasn't meant to be. *(Reflecting.)* Now, I sound like my father.

(Remembering.) He was so angry..."If I love him I'd just learn to...", but it is awful.

I'll never forget that first night. It was beautiful. Then snap. Even his kisses had that dead, smelly taste.

(Goes to the telephone.) Oh, well, I better start calling. *(She starts to pick up the receiver but doesn't.)* Jilted...just because I asked him to give up smoking. *(Hurt.)* Imagine, being in second place to a cigarette! I can't believe it! *(She moves downstage.)* I expected to have to compete against other women, we all do, but...a cigarette. *(Drifting.)* "Round and firm and fully packed." *(Realizing what she said.)* Where did I read...hear that? A cigarette something!?! I remember thinking "Round, firm, fully packed" sounded more like a woman than something you'd smoke. *(She shakes her head in disbelief. Crosses back to the telephone. Picks up the receiver.)* I guess I better start telling people.

(Looking at her wedding dress.) Maybe it is bad luck for a groom to see his bride in her wedding gown before the wedding.

(She dials the phone as the lights fade.)

As Usual

Originally AS USUAL was part of a comic trilogy BUSINESS AS USUAL, produced by Bread and Butter Dinner Playhouse.

Elizabeth Waring (Liz) is a sophisticated business woman who, in the past, has used her feminine wiles to achieve her business goals. She is tired of playing the game and being an "object for male attentions." She has, for about a year, seriously been looking for the right mister and is starting to be upset that all she can find is Mr. Wrong.

Trade conventions have an abundance of men, away from home and usually looking for the warmth of a one night stand. Working this convention, Liz has already had two dinner offers, both from married men, and five direct offers to fill someone's one night fantasy and it's only 11:00 AM on the third day of a five day conference -- so she's been telling her friend Irene.

LIZ. It was business. One of those boring trade conventions. Boring is not the right word to describe a trade convention. As long as we stay with business it's active. Right after we finish set up, the first day, the male population, which is usually four or five to one, gets the idea they're away from their wives and in heat. Usually they stop and talk, either watching us or -- surprise, possibly interested in the company. I'm a vice president. I shouldn't have to do this!

You act friendly, that's what we're here for, just selling the company, they'll come on strong: Dinner -- Show -- Cocktails...then watch out...your hotel or mine?...We're both away from home. It's always the same.

(Looking off.) Here he comes. It started...same as always...but...strange...I wanted him to ask. He just kept talking business. His eyes flashed as we spoke. You could feel him assessing everything. I hoped he'd get around to me, but he just kept talking business. I found myself running my hands through my hair. I fidgeted with my blouse buttons. My eyes wandered. *(Turns right.)* Lillian, please stop! Lillian had to interrupt, and she could just jabber on...he started to walk off. *(As if touching his shoulder.)* How long have you been doing this? Just in time, another second and he would have been swallowed by the crowd. I continued drawing him out. I figured if he'd talk, sooner or later he'd pick up or try to. What was that you said? Kids! Oh, shit! He's married. He just sparkles when he talks. Oh, so what if he's married? I don't really care! He's interesting. I'm all turned on and we're talking business. Oh no, he's drifting. Even if you just want a comparison or someone to sketch out shipments give me a call. I'd be happy to work up prices. *(Aside.)* To hell with a call. What about tonight? Why not now! Kids! Again! *(Excited.)* They're not your kids?!? Your brother's. Oh! *(Responding left.)* Jack, it's in the green file. *(Turning back.)* Where is he? Gone! I've got this empty space...a hole...*(She quickly rummages through her thoughts.)* Did I give him my business card when I said call? I usually do? Maybe he wasn't really interested. But, if he stopped for me, why did he leave...or leave that way? *(Rummaging around.)* I didn't even get his card. Maybe he wasn't so exciting. We probably wouldn't have hit it off. His eyes were nice but he really wasn't good looking. Who am I kidding? Sour grapes! Why didn't I ask him out? Why didn't I say something personal? Maybe, with all that business smart, he's really shy. It never happens the way...*(Right.)* Yes,

Lillian, I dropped some paper. Thank you. *(Trying to calm herself.)* Wasted! I wasted my opportunity. *(Bending over to pick up the...)* It's not paper. It's my business card! I must have dropped it...So I didn't give him a business card...*(Looking at the card.)* It's his business card! *(Excited.)* I've still got a chance!

A DISTANT VIEW

This play deals with the changing attitudes of a woman and her views on those changes. It was originally produced by the Hollywood Writers Collaboration opening April 10, 1972.

Susan Walker was the typical young woman, with loving parents, a perfect husband and a beautiful child. Everything life had to offer, she felt she had.

Married shortly after high school; she helped her husband through college and then set up housekeeping. As his salary started to move upwards, their lives were exactly what they wanted; a nice home and family. Tragedy struck and her husband of ten years, died. Part time jobs, minimum wage, working, going to school, and their limited insurance didn't give her and her young son much of the good life. There were other marriage offers; none that Susan wanted.

Susan now has to face the future; hers and her son's.

Susan is in her new European office. She doesn't know if she can handle the new job and relives the last few days.

SUSAN. It's been just a week. Tuesday! I knew Tuesday afternoon. They accepted me. I wasn't sure if I was happy or sad. But, I knew what I had to do.

I called Mom. She said she'd help. Three years...It's a long time.

Billy and I walked hand in hand as we entered the house. *(Smiling at the thought.)* Dad was delighted to see us. Billy and Dad were pals; in a moment they were playing. Dad was always great with children. *(Smiles broadly.)* He was great! I remember when we were kids...*(Reflecting.)* Dad never changes.

While Dad turned back the clock, Mom and I had our conversation. She was the level-headed one. Mom said it would be fine. She'd take Billy. *(Mock scolding.)* Dad thought I was wrong but he would be glad to have Billy with them. *(Lightly laughing.)* He certainly didn't want Billy left with anyone else. I love you Dad. *(Emotionally.)* I love you.

        (She crosses then stops.)

The tough part was yesterday morning. It was...*(Choking up.)* I was going to work in Europe. *(Regaining control.)* Great career move. When I got back at least I'd earn enough that Billy and I could live reasonably. The last year had been real hard, since Jim...my husband...

But now...three years away from my child was going to be...very difficult. Even if...I don't know...

After breakfast, Billy and I sat and talked. *(Talking to her son.)* "I have to go away for a while. I can't take you back with me. I'll be working in another country; when I come back I can give you more of the advantages we have not had. *(He doesn't understand.)* Billy, we need a better place to live; clothes, car, school..." He just looked at me. Watching him, I just wanted to cry. He asked if I loved him. "Oh, Billy. Of course I love you..." We had each other. I explained, "You will stay with your grandparents."

30

Billy looked up at me, his eyes saddened. "When will you come back?" he asked. The words choked in my mouth... "In three years." I tried to explain. "I will be far from here and I won't be able to visit. I must do this for both our sakes." He asked, "Is three years a long time?" *(Tears swell.)* I didn't know what to say.

He smiled at me as if trying to comfort me. "Don't worry about me, Mother," he said. "I'll be good." I hugged him...I didn't want to let go.

We said our goodbyes.

(She moves to her desk. Then looks up.)

I hope I made the right decision! —

(She returns to her work as the lights fade.)

[handwritten: Should she be trying to break herself away from the situation?]

[handwritten: Sarcasm louder more abrupt]

[handwritten: * "Three years... it's a long time" "Is three years a long time?" emphasis to portray its connection.]

Karen Flathers

LOVE IN THE MIND

Opened at the Broadway Playhouse in 1979 and was critically acclaimed as "A perfectly crafted modern day fairy tale."

Paula and John have been married for seven years and instead of an itch Paula is falling deeply, romantically, passionately in love with, of all people, her husband. She's dreaming of -- her husband. She's fantasizing about -- her husband. She is even enjoying the ordinary, such as watching him sleep.

John has slipped comfortably into complacency. Paula's amorous fire has sparked concern but no passion. He thinks something is wrong and schemes to find out what it might be. His scheming tittilates him and rekindles his flame. Both begin to feel something may be wrong with their marriage. Nothing's wrong! Everything is right. They are both in love!

PAULA. *(Enters. She looks off, almost dreaming. Then turns to her husband.)* John, I love you. *(She waits, then...)*

I know I don't say it often but I do love you.

(The response is not what she expected.) No. There's nothing wrong. I just had to say the words. *(She watches him.)* I know I'm silly. *(Laughing.)* You've told me often enough, how silly I am.

(Reacting.) Nothing's wrong! *(Confiding.)* I just had a strange night.

(Explaining.) Yes, in bed.

(Exasperated.) The same bed as you.

(Annoyed.) No, I didn't have a "bad" dream. *(Silly.)* I had a wonderful awake.

(Giggling.) Well, not quite awake.

(Answering.) You'll think it's silly.

Oh, alright. You don't usually sleep...I mean, I'm usually asleep before you...you know...on the way to the pillow and I'm asleep. Well, last night...yesterday you had a killer day...you were out before I even got to bed. You left your lamp on and when I went to turn it out I noticed you had this boyish grin...sleeping...just like you'd done something you shouldn't have. I found myself sitting in the chair watching you. It was like on our honeymoon...*(She tries to qualify.)* I didn't watch you on our honeymoon, I sort of...you know how it was...we shared it...Last night I just watched you sleep.

Not all night, just for a while. Oh, I don't know how long. I daydreamed...dozed...fantasized...fell more in love. *(Smiles at his comment.)* Some of that too. You curled your lips up and I just...*(Bubbly laughter.)*...yes, I did.

Seriously. So I kissed you. You didn't wake up. A couple of times I hoped you would wake and ravish me.

No. I didn't want to wake you...You were too beautiful, just sleeping. For some of it I'm not even sure I was awake myself. It might all be a dream. But, it was special. You were wonderful; Prince Charming! You rolled over and I crawled into bed, on my side, to watch you. I fell asleep. This morning, when I reached over, you were already out of bed. So here I am, spouting like a silly school girl; as her husband tries to get to work on time.

(Defensively.) I know. I'm silly.

See you tonight. *(She watches him exit. She turns and leans against the door.)* Men! *(Tickled.)* He'll never understand. So different. So much alike. I love him; with all my heart. I'd be so lost without him. *(She looks up -- spritely.)* Maybe it was a dream. Maybe...I think I'll go back to bed for some more. *(She crosses as the lights fade.)*

Goodluck with your monologue! you will do great! — AA.

Roslyn Witt

Secret Admirer

Originally performed on the same evening bill as LOVE IN THE MIND, the play won two playwriting awards; one from Players U.S.A. and the second from the Playwrights Foundation West.

Mrs. Willis ideally should have been a staff writer for the "I Love Lucy" show but the opportunity wasn't available to her. She settled for what she was expected to do -- marriage and children. Her family life didn't produce the right amount of excitement so Mrs. Willis was always willing to help life with a crazy idea. She enjoyed "helping" her neighbors.

In the following monologue, Mrs. Willis expresses her delightful method of interfering in her "friends" lives. She also unfolds the layers of veils that hide her own desires. There is so much more to this wonderful woman than just a nosey neighbor with a crazy scheme. She really does care.

MRS. WILLIS. *(Concerned.)* What do you mean you don't want to? But...but...we worked it all out. It's perfect. You changed your mind?

(Disappointed with the response.) So sudden! It's not sudden. You're just getting cold feet. You've worked on my idea for weeks, haven't you? *(Disappointed.)* Now you want to spoil everything. There's nothing to be afraid of. He'll never find out. Even if he did, he'd love you all the

more. Just consider this as a game...a marital game.
Foreplay, if you prefer.

So your husband has a temper. There's no man living
who hasn't got a temper, especially if you get him all
worked up. Take my word for it, this will work him up!

(Consoling.) Oh, don't worry. It will work. How do you
think I cured my husband of his neglect? I didn't like
being taken for granted.   Jealousy...and a little
competition... that's how. I sent myself valentines, subtle
at first. I even made like they were nothing and I didn't
care. Later I sent myself flowers and even gifts. One gift
was the laciest black negligee...*(She flutters and enjoys
the memory.)* The look on his face! *(Brushing off her
glow.)* I let him think that the cards and gifts were from
an old admirer.

Of course he exploded. Not at me...well, most of the
time...he boiled inside himself. He was so angry he
would pace and mutter. One evening he grabbed me like a
concubine and passionately devoured my mouth with
kisses. It was like being raped. Thrilling! Well...I was
too willing for rape. *(Changing her tone.)* But, I never let
on that there was no secret admirer. Even today, when I
get a card, he jumps up, "Who's that from?" *(Casually.)*
The whole game just brought us closer together. If I could
discuss it with him...*(Reacting sharply.)*   I never
would...but if I could, he'd probably agree; maybe even
thank me for the renewed excitement.

Now, don't be silly. Go ahead...like we planned. He'll
never find out. You'll have a wonderful time.

First the card; then at six I'll call.   You just
be...innocent. Go on. I'll see you later. *(She watches her
friend leave.)*

(Turning as if she is now alone.) I wish it was me. Oh, what excitement. *(Thinking. A smile lights up her face.)* Why not??!

(The lights fade.)

Sharon Gorrell Hoffman

UNREASONABLE EXPECTATIONS

This is a cutting from a segment of HOTEL, an evening of theatre. There were five segments: THE CLERK, ROOM 610, UNREASONABLE EXPECTATIONS, THE BELL BOY and ONE NIGHT STAND. HOTEL opened in 1971, performed for 22 performances and was abruptly closed by an Act of God.

Los Angeles had a 6.1 earthquake, after which the theatre on Melrose Avenue in Hollywood was closed for repairs. The theatre never opened again.

The various short one acts - segments - of HOTEL have appeared independently as parts of other One Act Play Evenings.

Sharon Harper is a very successful sales representative for National Computer Corporation. She is bright, attractive and efficient; ready at all times to sell her company's products. The president considers her a "sales fireball." Her sales abilities are unquestioned -- but personally Sharon has a slight selling problem -- she can't sell herself.

Sharon has reached that stage in life where her needs and desires seem to be changing. Her values previously emphasized business, wealth and position; now she just wants someone to share her life. She hasn't lost her interest in achievement; it's just that she'd also like to achieve a permanent male-female relationship. She might even consider time out for a child.

Returning from a sales conference, Sharon confronts herself, trying to discover why she can't be open and full of that special sales "quality" when it's not business.

SHARON. *(She shakes her head in confusion.)* I can't understand it. It's...I don't know. I'm no international sex goddess, but I don't think I look bad. *(She turns. Then again. Giggles.)* Not bad. I've even been told, once...no...*(Delighted.)*...twice, that I'm very attractive. *(Explaining.)* Now, I've never considered myself a shy person; I'm fairly comfortable in a crowd and I do well at a party, but, out of town...put me in a hotel and I'm alone.

It's like I'm invisible. I can see and hear everyone but no one sees me. Sometimes I can't even start a conversation with the hotel bartender. It's such an empty sensation. I don't know what to do.

I go to the meetings, we have lunch, occasionally dinner with a client...but alone. I never meet that someone special. Actually, I never meet anyone.

I find myself watching more television on a five day business trip than I'd see in five months at home. There is nothing on television and it seems even worse when you're out-of-town. I find myself watching re-runs and bad late night movies.

Occasionally I'll get daring. I get dressed to kill and go out alone to a local nightclub or hotel lounge, wander the tourist spots...I always think maybe tonight but I really don't expect...Usually I feel so lonely and I have all that work back at the hotel that when somebody does say something I head out and back to my room. *(She thinks, then giggles.)* Once, I found myself riding up and down in the hotel elevator in hopes of meeting someone. I made eleven trips, then one of the bellmen asked me if there was a problem. I was so embarrassed, I got off at the next floor and walked up nine floors to my room. In Chicago I tried the elevator again - because I saw this cute guy - It got stuck. Naturally, he got off on two. Five hours before they could get me out...between the 3rd and 4th floors.

I do get opportunities...an attractive man will start a conversation, another will smile needing encouragement...I just can't and when I do...it's all wrong!

I don't believe I have unreasonable expectations. I'm not looking to fall in love. I don't want to be swept off my feet or expect rockets to burst with a first kiss. *(Then for the first time, she realizes.)* You know, maybe...maybe that's exactly what I am waiting for! I want a white knight to sweep me off my feet, carry me away, and love me forever.

(Shaking her head in disbelief.) I don't believe I said that. All these years! I'm the practical businesswoman! What utter nonsense. I'm waiting for a knight on a white horse...Prince Charming...Happily Ever After...Practical? Not me! I'm an incurable romantic.

(Walking off.) I wonder if he'll find me? At least I know what I'm looking for - Prince Charming. *(Turns to audience. Smiling.)* Maybe my next trip. *(Exits.)*

Amy Ardavany

P.O.V.

The Play (POINT OF VIEW) was first performed at Keesler Air Force Base in Biloxi, Mississippi, April 11, 1964. It ran for five weeks. Six years later, May 15, 1970 extensively rewritten, and retitled P.O.V., it opened at the Players Theatre in Hollywood. This time it ran for two years; was critically acclaimed and received ENTERTAINMENT WEEKLY's Best Play Award.

Dana Wilcox is the kind of woman who could have everything or anything she wants. A bright, personable, very attractive woman, Dana could talk her way into and out of any situation. Most people give in, rather than argue with her.

Men, boys when she was younger, just seem to adore Dana. Regardless of what and how she says things, even when she's abrasive, they don't take offense. Dana has that winning way and men enjoy being with her, even if they don't agree with what she says. Her husband, John, a macho male, agreed to all of Dana's premarital requests, regardless of how foolish he thought most of them were.

Dana left a good job to marry John; she was successful in business. Now she considers herself the perfect mother and totally in control of all situations -- at least that's what she thought.

The following cutting catches Dana at that moment when she relives some memories and realizes the truth. She takes her discovery with a positive attitude.

DANA. *(Strong and proud.)* I remember how I always bested the boys; in all the games they wanted to win, I won! They were so strong, yet I was more able...so smart, but my grades were better. When we would wit, mine was sharper. *(Very proud.)* I always managed the last word. *(Remembering.)* My mother scolded me...*(Mimicking.)* and advised it was not my place. What place was mine? My Aunt Lil tried to get me to be like her. She always gave in to Uncle Jack and my dad. I always knew Aunt Lil was wrong. She shouldn't have been Uncle Jack's slave. *(Adamant.)* I wasn't going to be like my mom or Aunt Lil. By the time I was ten, I knew I wasn't ever going to let any man be my "master!" For a while I thought I was the only woman who had these feelings but by the time I was in high school there was a whole movement. Women all around were showing men that they could lead...and do it better. It was marvelous. Showing those supercilious pants-wearers that they weren't supermen...just men. A mere woman could do everything thay did and do it better. We even got TV shows and films with women as heroes. Boy, how they complained.

I was a Ms. instead of a Miss. I didn't let them take the credit when I did the work. I was the first woman, at 27, to be a vice president in a men's shoe company.

I met John. We agreed to share our lives. I was no chattel; *(Strong.)* he knew we were partners. We agreed to work together side by side. Sometimes he would be first and at other times I would walk ahead. He had to know that...this was the way it should be. We were equals!

(She laughs lightly. Her mood lightens.)

What fickle nonsense my ideas. *(Warmly.)* My first born was a girl, then a boy and another boy; they were wonderful. Just watching them was pure joy. I could see my daughter's strength; like me, she excelled. I thought the cycle was to repeat itself. All those years, fighting to

46

survive...to prove I was his equal...his better. *(Laughing.)* What foolishness! I never proved anything. I made a good mother, but he was by far a better father than I could ever be. I found myself the weaker sex, for my love, though he tried to share, had actually conquered. *(She raises her head to look up.)* I'm sorry, Aunt Lil. *(Tears swell inside of her.)* You were right. I'm not his equal...and I never will be. I don't really want to be his equal. *(Reflecting.)* I want to be held; cared for; loved. *(She takes a deep breath.)* I'm...just a woman...*(Smiling.)* and I love being a woman. I even love being his possession. *(She laughs gently at herself, as the lights fade.)*

Paula Hoffman (Landes)

FINAL MOMENT

This monologue is from the Musical Review EVERY LADY originally performed at the Gate Theatre in Hollywood. EVERY LADY is a collection of stories, monologues, scenes and songs, all light-hearted moments in the lives of four women.

All the information that we know about Wendy is here, in the monologue. The actress should use this information as the character outline and bring to the monologue moments of her own life that can blend with the character to complete the characterization. If you feel that personal moments are still insufficient then add to the outline creative moments.

WENDY. Here it is, the greatest day of my life, everything I have waited and saved for...the dreams, fantasies, and all those moments of growing up, finally at their peak. *(She seems to glow with the memories swimming around in her head.)* When I was in the second grade there was David; in the fourth there was Bobby; fifth and sixth there was John Wilcox, he was sooo cute...*(Remembering.)* Junior High was the pits. *(Getting angry.)* Janet Felton, that witch; she was hopeless. The only girl I knew who budded out in the sixth grade. By the seventh grade she had every boy oggling her...oh, those boys. I didn't have a real date for all of Junior High! *(Her anger fades.)* High School was different. *(Smiling.)* Janet didn't get all that much and when the word got out that she padded what little she had...well...My mom would say I was a "late bloomer." *(Admiring her own shape.)* I finally filled out. *(She turns showing off her figure.)*

Paula Hoffman (Landes)

Joey chased me for three years., I nearly lost him to that silly brunette. He had her, but he wasn't going to have me...not like that. *(Rambling on, as she combs her hair.)* I dated the four most popular boys and then there was Billy. Joey was green with envy. He was so sure that I was going to make love to Billy; for a while so was I. I used to get so hot and so curious. Oh, how I wanted him. Or...just wanted to do it. I don't know. If it wasn't for Billy's reputation he would have had me. I wasn't going to be *just* another conquest. I wanted to be something special. Every time Billy scored...a few weeks later he had a new girl...he did say I was different...*(She smiles.)* Joey was great...the way I let him take me away from Billy, was wonderful! I think Billy knew and just played along, but it was everything I'd ever expected it to be. I was dressed in white, a virgin goddess...I got to slip into a sexy negligee, and finally give myself to Joey. Married! He waited and he is ready. I am really ready! This is it! *(She spins around in what seems to be ecstasy. Stopping suddenly.)* I'm not going to do it! I won't be a virgin sacrifice. I'm going to stay right here in this bathroom until...what am I going to do? I don't want to go to bed with him...Billy, yes...but...*(Thinking.)* Joey looks cute, but...*(Looking around.)* There has got to be a way out of here. *(Discouraged.)* I should have listened to my Dad. He didn't think Joey was right for me. *(Hopelessly trapped. She sits.)* I waited all my life for this opportunity and what I really want now...is...a Headache!

GOOD NIGHT

The Best Time cutting from GOOD NIGHT was originally cut for an audition at ABC. The actress needed a short monologue in which she could demonstrate a full range of acting abilities.

GOOD NIGHT originally previewed at the West Coast One Act Festival Presentations. It received a second place award and was later produced by Players U.S.A.

Billie Harper is a loving daughter. Her mother was always there but they were never really close. Billie's father was the all important figure, to both mother and daughter. When her father died Billie drifted away. After Billie married, she'd bring her daughter to visit "Gran" but there was still that distance.

At 2:30 pm Billie got a call, she dutifully responded. By 4:00 pm she was at the hospital. For the first time, mother and daughter really communicated.

BILLIE. When the phone rang I was knee deep in everything. Barbara had her dolls everywhere, the cake was in the oven, I had two loads of wash going, the vacuum out and Jim would be back tomorrow. Jim, my husband, had to fly up north on business.
(She turns, picks up the phone and talks.)
Mom...Mom...What's the matter? You're where? Of course I'll come. I'll be there as soon as possible. *(She hangs up the phone.)*
It took me thirty minutes to clean up, dress and find someone that could keep Barbara. I caught a cab and got to the hospital just before four. I didn't expect to be long.

Mom and I didn't have much to say to each other. We were never very close.

It was a long night. *(She takes an instant to reflect then smiles. Gently.)* Definitely among the best times I've ever had. She was rare company. *(Her enthusiasm builds.)* Bright...Funny...Warm...So full of life! For seven hours we talked, non-stop. *(Bubbling.)* We never argued, not once. I'm sure that's some kind of record...at least for us. *(Excited.)* She told stories...*(Giggling.)* they were so funny...about when I was little, oh I'd heard most of them before, but for the first time she actually told them to me. *(Tearful.)* I loved every minute of it. In the past, I was just there, or I would hear someone re-tell the story that she had told them. *(Excited.)* This was different. It was...wonderful! We relived some of her memories about my father, their love and her most precious moments with him. *(Touched.)* She even shared some of their intimacies with me. She loved Dad so...so much. We were never as close as we were this night. We'll never be that close...again. *(Tickled.)* We laughed like school girls, cackling and giggling in a conspiratorial manner. It was special. So special. I always wanted to be close to her. Last night we were as close as we could be. *(Crying.)* It was perfect!

(Regaining her composure.) I was so tired and she had so much energy...so much life...I don't believe I will ever be able to properly express how perfect this time was. I was exhausted as the sun came up. At one point I think I was giggling and I'm not sure if I was awake or asleep. *(Remembering a beautiful moment.)* At another time I caught a glimpse of her watching me doze...she was so gentle...finally, she fell asleep. *(Her voice wavers. Her emotions swell.)* She needed the rest. She was so peaceful. It was only a minute or two...so fast...then...she was gone. *(Trying to compose herself but unable to hold back the tears.)* I love my mother...loved her dearly. Hearing her talk...listening...she made it so easy...so beautiful. *(Crying.)* I'm going to miss her.

HIS

HIS AND HERS was a two person show designed to take a young couple through the trials and tribulations of a modern marriage.

Rita and Jason have reached a point of total impass. He has been unfaithful, caught, and has decided to divorce Rita to marry his young new love. He uses several excuses about his career and their life but she only sees a replay of her mother's life and relates her discontentment.

The scene originally was placed in the kitchen of their home, any setting will work adequately.

RITA. *(She stands, staring off. She turns out. Annoyed, she boils over.)* You feel you missed your chance; your career isn't going the way you expected...but, you have your career. What about me?! *(She takes a breath to regain her composure.)* I wanted to be a doctor. I was pre-med, when we started dating. I settled for a teaching job to help you finish Law School. I didn't want to end up like my mother. She settled for my father, and when he turned fifty, he left. *(Hurt.)* Mom just never had anything after that. I wanted something better. *(Gently smiling and remembering.)* Then you winked at me...do you remember...*(Her tone lightens as she speaks.)* I still remember the way your eyes flashed and that silly little grin. I was hooked. I guess I still am. *(Joking.)* It took over a year for me to get you to propose. *(Curious.)* Would you have married me if I went to bed with you? *(Panicking; she might get the wrong answer.)* Don't answer! I don't really want to know. *(Relaxing.)* Do you remember how you promised, after you finish Law School,

I go to Medical School? It didn't happen that way did it? Your dad died; you took over the practice, your mom got sick, you were always too busy when I'd ask about Medical School. "Later...later" you'd say. Then we had two kids...I never got to Med School. All I got was a permanent job as your housemaid; a never-ending stack of laundry and dirty dishes. If I'm not satisfied I'm not left with much in the way of alternatives. I could go back and teach third grade. I didn't like it when I put you through Law School and I certainly wouldn't like it now. You see, your career is real and it's still going forward but mine never got started. *(Realizing.)* *My* career...actually my whole life just became an extension of yours; your wife and the mother of your children. I guess I lost...No, I gave you...my identity. *(Smiling.)* I guess all I've got to look forward to are hot flashes, menopause, gray hair and sagging skin. *(Exasperated.)* If I didn't love you so much...but I do...I love that silly grin and I still go all to pieces when you wink at me. *(Her mind jumps back to...)* Although you don't wink at me much these days. Doing it all over from the beginning, I'd probably make the same stupid mistakes my mother did. I'd trade my career...for your love.

I do love you and I probably always will. Like my father, you're leaving, not for the same reasons...you're leaving for your career...but I'm still left with nothing. I couldn't understand my mother's plight then, but I can now. Given a chance for love against anything else, we'll pick...love. *(She looks off. Then back with a remorseful tear.)* For a woman it's a good choice -- LOVE.

PART II

This section consists of monologues that can be used in varying lengths to meet several audition circumstances.

Sharon Gorrell Hoffman

LAST ADVENTURE

The following two monologues are cut from THE LAST ADVENTURE, which opened at Theatre Unique in New York City.

Each monologue will stand as a short character audition piece. Both cuttings can be put together to create a longer piece. The joining of the two monologues will also create a wider range of characterization for the actress to present.

Christine is a rare individual. She has the warmth and inner beauty we all seem to search for. She has always been afraid to live the life of her dreams; unselfishly sacrificing her own desires for the benefit of those she loved. There is no regret or sour grapes in her sacrifices -- only love.

Now Christine is about to do everything she has ever wanted to do. She is thrilled and delighted at her courageous stand and the adventure that lays before her. But the underlying reason eventually dampens her spirits.

I

A WONDERFUL TIME

CHRISTINE. *(An attractive woman. Dressed very conservatively, maybe a bit dowdy. She is wearing plain rim glasses. Her hair style seems a little old for her years, the long hair tied up in a simple bun. Our first impression is a quiet spinster woman.)* I think I'm going to do it. It's time I got away from this...Ever since I can remember I've had dreams of traveling. I haven't. I've always been afraid: first, afraid of what Mother would think; then afraid that sister wouldn't like it; the last couple of years I've been concerned that the people at work wouldn't approve. I've spent more time wondering what other people think than what really matters. Well, it's time for me...for what I need. *(She removes her glasses.)* I have booked a world excursion, spared no expense, and...I am going to try to enjoy myself. A two month cruise, ten weeks in the Orient, and a six week party across Europe...No, I don't know when I'm coming home...*(Hesitating.)* Maybe...I'll see...*(Excited.)* This is something I never thought I'd ever have the nerve to do. Now, I'm going to do it! *(She removes the clip holding her bun and her hair falls about her shoulders.)* How am I paying for it? *(Glibly.)* With everything. That's what this is, an everything trip. I've cleaned out my savings, traded in my pension, sold my car, furniture and the rest...credit cards. For once in my life I'm going all the way. *(She fluffs her hair and it is obvious that this is an attractive woman.)* Farewell Miss Practical. *(She rearranges her outfit; removes the neck ribbon, opens her top button, flips the collar up.)* Hello Francine Fashion. *(She spins around.)* I'm on my way. *(Calling off, as if to the whole world.)* Look out, here comes Francine. *(She crosses. Stops. Turns.)* Good bye.

If you are combining the two monologues -- after "Good bye" Christine crosses -- stops and looks out. Then continues with the dialogue. You can either disregard the suitcase reference or use it as the connection. She would then cross to the suitcase and...Her tone changes rapidly. The light air gives way to the pain that weighs heavily on her heart.

Paula Hoffman (Landes)

II

FINALLY

(She stops...looks out.) The change? There's no change.
I've always planned on traveling. I just never found the
time. *(Hiding something.)* I've waited and saved...now
it's time...to enjoy. *(She tenses, trying to restrain her
emotions.)* I have to do something...*(In a half-hearted
joke.)*...before it's too late. I don't want to wait until I'm
one of those senior ladies with silver hair. I
can't...I...*(She turns.)* Yes, I...I saw the doctor. The tests
were...the same...they were fine. *(She crosses; again
regaining her composure. Rambling.)* It's not the way I
expected...this trip...it will be my
chance...fun...*(Uncovering her feeling.)* I thought, by
now, I'd have a family. I always saw myself...a
husband...children...two boys...*(Again, a sudden change
of thought.)* If I got sick...sick...my sister...I love her
but...she'd help...she'd take care of me...I would never
hear the end of how much she did. Never, until...I'd rather
be alone! She wouldn't even allow me that. Everyone
would hear how much she did, for her sister. I wouldn't
have a shred of self-respect...she'd milk the situation until
I would feel so guilty...I'd even feel bad for her...I
couldn't take that. *(Remembering.)* Funny, as kids I
envied her...I guess I still do...she got so much...so much
at my expense...even married my only boyfriend...I
loved him so...*(Holding back the tears.)* This trip is my
answer...my chance...first class...the very best of
everything. *(She chuckles.)* Buried in debt. I'm going to
be buried...buried...*(Cynically.)* I don't think we're ever
ready. *(Scared.)* I don't want to die. I don't want to die!
(She cries.)

Divorce Conflict

The three monologues that follow are short cuttings from DIVORCE CONFLICT. The 1979 opening at the Broadway Playhouse was hailed, by SHOWCASE, as "an evening of pure enjoyment."

Each monologue, titled for simplicity, depicts a different moment in time as Constance Standard (Connie) realizes what she has done and why. If a short acting piece is needed any one of the three could be presented. All three can be used as a single performance monologue or they can be used in pairs to produce a medium length monologue.

The versatility of having three short performance pieces that can be interrelated for different lengths gives a performer a very useful tool. On a moment's notice the performer can prepare a monologue of different time lengths and show different aspects of a single characterization.

Connie is a modern woman, well educated and truly capable of getting exactly what she wants -- even if it isn't what she really does want.

I

NINE YEARS

CONNIE. (*Enters. She is attractive and extremely neatly dressed. She opens her purse; takes out a tissue and blots her lips. Turns...*) So, it's over. A drive downtown, forty-five minutes in a government building, six of the coldest people I have ever met and here I am. *(She crosses down. Sad.)* I got everything...everything I wanted. No complications. *(She reflects for a second.)* Nine years older, I don't think any wiser, and I'm basically back where I was. *(She paces, right.)* It was so simple...different...I guess I expected more...at least something...I don't feel any different. Maybe they should make us do it all backwards. Of course, if that was to work, I'd probably have to do another nine years, in reverse. *(Thinking out loud.)* If I could stop for the good times...*(Mischievously.)* Maybe I could do it like a VCR, fast reverse. *(Playful.)* Then I could stop and replay just the good times. There were quite a few. *(Laughs. She sits.)* You know I'm sure all of the important issues are meaningless now. *(Half heartedly.)* I wanted to be my own woman. *(Disgusted.)* What utter nonsense. All that, I'm being smothered...dominated...used...*(Drifting.)* Less than two hours and it's all over. Nine years of the best man I've ever known...the only man I've ever loved...and now...I'm divorced.

II

MOMENTS

(Composing herself.) I remember growing up. All I ever thought about was finding that right man, getting married, raising a family...being like my mother...living happily ever after. Then the wedding came; all white and flowery...oh, it was a happy time. My family, his...*(Fondly.)* my dad was *(A quiet thought. Smile.)* ...Then the honeymoon...it really was all that I had expected. *(Her mood changes. Defensive.)* Young women believe that nonsense. *(A split second of*

reflection.) Oh, it's not nonsense. It's beautiful! Finding that perfect someone to share your life...being in love. *(Gently touching herself. Remembering.)* Touching. All the comfortable quiet moments...nothing going on, he's there, you're there...apart but together. I wouldn't trade those feelings for a world of feminist equality. I don't want to be a modern woman. *(Colorful.)* I don't want to open my own doors. I like being on a pedestal. *(Giggling.)* I don't even care if they pay me less than him; I'll get him to buy dinner and pay for the tickets. *(Wryly.)* Where is all this leading? *(Realizing.)* Oh, no! *(Happy.)* I'm going to make a very stupid mistake.

III

ONCE MORE

He didn't want the divorce. He didn't want to fight. *(Tears swell.)* He just wanted me to be happy. *(Holding the tears back.)* I guess that's all he ever wanted. *(Thinking.)* What did I want? Why did I put us both through this? When we left the court, he kissed me..."stay in touch", he said...*(Realizing.)* Oh, no! That crazy fool...he still loves me. *(Understanding.)* He's not crazy...I am...I was just feeling unwanted. I put us through all of this, just because of my pride? *(Exasperated.)* I love him, too. *(Lightly.)* I got us into this mess, now, I've got to get us out. *(Delightfully scheming.)* I could seduce him. He never could resist me. *(Returning to reality.)* I never could resist him either. *(Confident.)* I'm going to call him. I can't call him, not two hours after we're divorced. *(Considering.)* Why not!? Why wait?! He loves me and I love him. He may not know that yet but...It's worth another chance. *(Enthusiastically.)* I'd love to get married, again!

ON THE SHELF

The two monologues that follow are both from ACT II of ON THE SHELF. The monologues can be used independently or together. Again they have been titled for simplicity.

Catherine is a very plain but attractive woman. She is careful about her appearance and orderly about her life. Everything has a time and a place. She has worked hard to reach her status in life and feels that now is the time for a man and marriage. But, she has been totally unable to find a man that fits her expectations. She always believed that he would appear in good time. She has been looking for this perfect male companion for much too long a period. No one seems to fit her version of *Perfect*.

By accident, Catherine meets Walter, a young man whose attitude fits that of a much more mature person. They seem to be Mr. & Mrs. Perfect, except that Catherine has severe difficulty with the criticism from friends and family about Walter's age.

Catherine has made up her mind to give up this *unnatural* relationship. She feels that a man of Walter's age and a woman of her age do not belong together. She will have to find someone else; someone the *right* age.

It is very important to understand that although Catherine wants to marry Walter, she would give him up. She would rather be proper than happy. It has always been extremely important to her, what other people think.

After an unusually bad day Catherine finds herself sorting out the problems. Talking to herself, she decides what is the right course of action.

Any room or place will do for the setting.

I

TIMELY

CATHERINE. *(Stands. Paces. The words are, at first, verbalizations of her thoughts.)* How could I allow this to happen? I...I've always been a very quiet woman. *(Commenting.)* Sometimes too quiet. I expected to get married after college. Oh, I told myself that I was looking for a fling...I wasn't...I wanted to settle down. It didn't happen that way. The sexual revolution exploded around me and I found life a little too fast. In some ways I was just scared...most of the time I was scared. *(Lightly.)* I kept looking for Mr. Right. No luck in that department. I do keep trying. I'm with the same company, working steady, since I got out of school. Occasionally, I meet someone...dinner, date...sometimes we go out a couple of times...it never seems to go anywhere. They try to bed me, but, I...well...even at my age I'm still looking for a wedding ring. Maybe it means I'll never...at least I thought...oh, I don't know. *(Deciding.)* I see myself as a wife. *(Resigned.)* If I can't be a wife then I'll be an old maid...alone...Then this boy started. Ten years younger than I am. It was flattering. Nothing of any consequence but fun. My friends...*(Colorful.)*...and my mother! I didn't handle that too well. *(Defensive.)* It was just his infatuation. That's what I thought at first. I was wrong. He's been a gentleman...handled everything the correct way or at least the way I always thought a man and a woman should go about falling in love. *(Painfully.)* I know other women are doing it...maybe it's the style....but I feel I'm robbing the cradle. What are people going to think? What is my family going to say? I can hear my mother! Now he's proposed; one knee, a ring...told everyone. It is absolutely everything I have ever dreamed about. He is Mr. Right, except for his age. *(Decisively.)* I just cannot marry him.

II

PREROGATIVE

I'm not going to play mother and wife to a younger man. I've always felt it was ludicrous when an older man tries to recapture his youth with a young woman. But I can accept an older man...*(Thoughtful.)* What is the difference? *(Snickering.)* Maybe it's because our bodies seem to fall apart faster than theirs do. *(Amorous thought.)* His body is beautiful. He's so full of life. His eyes...his smile...I would like to...*(Her body vibrates with the thought.)* Fantasy is not reality. It just could not work. When I'm sixty he'd be fifty...probably chasing after thirty year olds. *(Faltering.)* What am I talking about? We've got all those years getting to fifty and sixty. Am I going to settle for lonely old maid...oh, what the hell! Who cares what people think? I'm going to marry that young man. *(She turns to exit. Stopping. Turns back.)* I'm going to make us both very happy. *(She exits.)*

ENCOURAGEMENT

This two person One Act Play was first presented at the Hollywood Center Theatre as part of an evening of one acts. The play was selected as a finalist for the Playwrights Theatre One Act Competition in 1971. Later that year, I mounted a one woman version of the play as part of an evening of "Performances by Women" that I produced and directed for The West Coast Actors Group.

The following monologues are taken from a later version rewritten for a tour by Players U.S.A.

Dotty Howard has her sixth appointment with a psychiatrist. She knew she needed help because everyone told her she did...so she went...

Each of the following short monologues depicts a different image and emotional moment that Dotty is trying to express. Her need to explain and justify her actions to a third party is strongly counterpointed with her need to accept herself. Whether or not she needs this doctor or that there really is a problem remains undecided. The cutting can subtextually develop in several ways; primarily, she doesn't need help and seeing this doctor is a waste of time or she definitely is having a psychological breakdown. For rehearsal purposes it is interesting to develop both of the above facets; then see where they take you.

If the character appeals to you and a longer monologue is needed then consider combining two or all three of these monologues to develop the desired length.

I

AFRAID

(Dotty crosses to the desk.) I don't feel like doing the couch thing. Is it alright if I just sit, or...Thank you.

(Dotty sits. She is uncomfortable and trying to act relaxed.) I've always been afraid...Afraid of almost everything. My desires are unending. *(Qualifying.)* No, I'm not talking about those desires. *(She hesitates.)* Well, maybe? No. I mean the desire to do things; to be important, to be exciting -- to be noticed! Let me clarify by example. When I was in High School, most of my friends wanted to get married, that was their main goal -- that was it! There were a few girls that wanted to go to college; I don't know if they wanted to get married. Going to college was the important part; it made them important. They were "IN"; they were the leaders; they were going to college. So I wanted to go.

I mustered all my courage, which really isn't much, and started college. It went well. *(Responding.)* No. Not too well. I lasted about three weeks. I was scared to death. The whole college idea scared me. No...The boys scared me. They were aggressive... They weren't boys; they were men. I was still a girl...and very immature at that.

I grabbed a marriage proposal from a guy I didn't really want and left school. Want! David wasn't even pleasant. I dated him occasionally in High School...when I didn't have a date. The last resort before you make excuses to your friends that you don't want to go because you're *(Overacting.)* ...too tired, very sick, or something...

I know I didn't love him. I don't even think I liked him. He did ask. I married him! I might have had the sense not to get married, but everyone said it was a mistake, so naturally I had to prove them wrong. *(Realizing.)* I wouldn't have had the sense, I would have had to admit I was wrong. *(A fleeting thought.)* My sister! I just couldn't give her that much power over me...I couldn't.

II

MARRIED

(Composing herself.) So we got married! Now, I was going to have the best marriage. Perfect sex. Perfect love. Perfect home. Perfect children. Everyone would envy us. *(Shaking her head in disbelief.)* No one did. It was awful!

It started all right, but...oh, it wasn't all right. It was a mess. I know better now. But   looking back... Honeymoon...love...sex...I remember lying there after, thinking, "This is what I waited for?" We didn't even kiss that first time. My nightgown...it never came off. He left his pajamas on. All we did was rumple the bed clothes. *(Hurt.)* It was over! He went to sleep. We didn't even talk. *(Emotional.)* I lied there trying to...*(She can't finish the words. Slowly she composes herself.)*

Well, if that's what it was, then we'd be the best. I told everybody it was the best marriage. *(Over acting,)* "Love making is unbelievable -- better than I ever dreamed." *(Serious.)* I lied. I just kept lying...to myself, the family...friends...Life was terrible and it got worse.

Nine years...*(Shaking her head in disbelief.)* Nine...I never got my nightgown off...never. I never saw him completely naked. If an instant flash was passionate excitement -- I think I had one or two -- maybe! We could "make love" during a single TONIGHT SHOW commercial.

(She turns.) I'm getting to it!

Well, after we got divorced I went out on my own. Well, not quite. I was 29 and my parents were still propping me up.

One collection of second-rate, go nowhere, do nothing jobs. I was headed right back into the same mold. Afraid of doing anything. I would have found another husband and...and nothing. A loser. That's what I attract. Losers.

But I found him. *(Explaining.)* I think, that was, he found me...picked me up...*(Chuckles.)* I hate the sound of that, but it's true. He picked me up in a bar. I was so afraid of being a one-night stand -- the week after our night -- that I was afraid to miss his call for fear he wouldn't call back. God, if he didn't call!

(Returning to the story.) That first night! I was overwhelmed. He was brash, outspoken, beautiful, elegant, debonnair, exciting, wonderful...He was everything I ever read and fantasized and more. He was the best I'd ever known or dated, or...Why he picked me I'll never know, but he did, although I thought for sure I was going to lose him; at least two or three times in that first couple of hours.

(She stops for another comment.) I know. I'm drifting. I'll try to stay on topic.

Now he's there. Maybe a father figure. Definitely a lover. What am I saying? I don't know anything about psychology. But, he's here. *(Pointing to herself.)* Here!

He says I can do it.

(Responding.) Do anything! Doesn't matter what it is. If he says I can do it, then I want to do it, for me, to prove he's right, to be one of the important people. I want to be the best.

(She waits for approval, but nothing...)

III

UNVEILED

(Dotty crosses to the window, opens the blinds and stares out. After a moment, she turns, and...)

Does it make sense to you now? Don't look at me with that blank stare.

(Crosses to the edge of the desk.) I just spent five bloody minutes pouring my heart out, while you listened as if you were asleep. I don't think you understand. I don't think you ever will. You don't care!

You see. I am a woman. I need him. I'm not really complete. Maybe some women are, but I'm not. I'm not a feminist and I certainly don't want to be equal. Oh, maybe I could do these things on my own. Maybe I could. But with him, I can, and I love it. With him, I'm the best. He may not see it, but I am the best and I'm not going to lose him. Because with him everything is better than it ever was. I'm better and I can be even better. Without him, it would be like it was before...empty. *(She listens for a moment, then gets angry again.)* You just don't see it! You are a bloody fool. I am a woman who needs a man. I'm not self-sufficient. Regardless of what everyone thinks, I will never be a macho woman. Maybe I was born out of my time. I'm Victorian. I want to be soft and gentle and protected. I want to be his...Maybe that's wrong by today's standards or maybe I'm part of a small group, because there are others like me, and just maybe we are right. It doesn't really matter, right or wrong. The important thing is, I need his help. I want him. *(With a great big, warm, sensual smile.)* I'm a woman. *(Glowing.)* I love him.

THE CLOUD

Originally written for submission to the International One
Act Festival.   It was one of five one acts selected for
production.

Roz Martin is a waitress in a small cafe on the east side
of New York.   Her life is grey, plain, and very ordinary;
she works, goes home and takes care of her sick
grandmother.   There has never been much, that could be
considered fun, in her life.

Today a very pleasant elderly man had coffee and a
pretzel at the cafe.   Business was slow and he talked to
Roz.   This elderly man set into motion discontent in Roz's
life.   Now she wanted more than what she has.

On the way home, this very quiet woman, talked to
herself.   When she reached home she told her grandmother
what happened.

The cutting below is a mixture of reality and fantasy.
We don't know if it actually took place or, if it did,
whether or not it was real or just in Roz's mind.   We also
don't know who or what was the elderly man.   We do
know that everything has and will continue to change for
Roz.   She is on the verge of transforming from a grey
caterpillar to a flaming red butterfly.   Life will no longer be
dominated by the dull day-to-day tedium; it will become a
continuously stimulating adventure.

I

LIFE

ROZ. *(Entering.)* Nan, I'm home! Nan...

(Cut off but being polite.) Yes, it was a glorious day.

Different? Yes, I do...yes...I feel very different.

(Full of excitement and anxious to tell her story.) I've got to tell this to someone. I'm just going to burst. *(Trying unsuccessfully, to compose herself.)* There I was, standing on 45th and Broadway. It was an insane situation. I'd never believe anything like it could happen...it did?! I certainly don't know how I'm going to convince anyone else. I don't know why I should try...but I'm going to...I have to...I've got to tell you what happened. *(Replaying the earlier event.)* Forty-fifth and Broadway. This is usually a crowded and active area at 5:30. This evening was no different; people going everywhere, in every direction. I stepped back, close to a shop window, and watched the movement. *(Reflecting.)* I guess I just like to feel the excitement of New York., It's fun to watch the people...*(Resuming her own excitement at telling the story.)* The street had the feeling of a Western movie cattle stampede -- if someone fell, they'd be finished, trampled into the ground by the herd. *(Her tone changes and excitement seems to subside.)* At first, I didn't notice...then this strange cloud...it just drifted overhead. The people slowed and stopped...I mean just stopped and looked up. Even the cars slowed...and then traffic came to a halt. Drivers got out of their cars...horns blared...then it quieted...peaceful...*(Smiling.)* We were all just watching this beautiful pink cloud. At the time, I didn't think there was anything unusual about a pink cloud. But as I told you, the more I think about this, the more ludicrous it becomes. So we're standing there watching this pink

cloud, people are chatting politely, giggling and just being extremely friendly. A cab driver, a New York City Cab Driver, gets out of his cab, picks up some trash in the street and puts it into the trash basket; several hoodlums, one with blue hair, the other looks like the leader of the skulls gang, help this elderly man find a comfortable seat on a bench. It is unbelievable! But then it was right. *(Gently smiling.)* People just being nice. Everyone liked and respected each other; they were being helpful and friendly. As far as I could see, the city, in every direction was coming to a halt; more and more poeple were caught in the aura of this - pink cloud. If this continued, New York City would become known as the nicest city in the world, for a while it was so nice. One lovely lady expressed her feelings, which summed it up beautifully, she simply said: "I've never felt so good and it's wonderful to see everyone so happy. I wish everyone in the world could feel this way." *(Everything changes; her tone, excitement, intensity.)* Then it was gone. The pink cloud drifted away. The crowd moved, the car horns blared, people screamed, and cursed, and no one cared...It was as if it...never happened. *(Reacting to disbelief.)* Don't look at me like that! I told you, you wouldn't believe me. But it did happen, and I'm not going to forget it! *(She takes a breath and exhales. Sadly.)* It was the most beautiful moment I'd ever known.

I told you I felt different. Wonderfully different.

If you're going to use ENTHUSIASM without LIFE, start the monologue with the last line, above, "I...wonderfully different."

II

ENTHUSIASM

When? I don't know. It just...On the way home, like I told you. Everything was so strange, wonderful, exciting...I just...No! No! I think it all started...yes, it did! *(Realizing.)* At the shop. The old man! That's when it started; right after he came in.

(Again exploding with a renewed burst of enthusiasm.)

Nan, right after lunch, we got quiet in the shop, like we do everyday. I usually busy myself by cleaning up and getting ready for tomorrow's breakfast. Well, I was working when he came in and sat at the counter by my station.

A nice old man, so I didn't ask him to move. I don't usually serve customers there that late in the day. All he wanted was a coffee and pretzel.

...Grey beard, rather round...you know, too heavy...*(Remembering.)* Old suit...He had a really wonderful smile. Warm. You could say anything and not feel uncomfortable. We talked.

About...*(Unsure.)*...what I was doing...things.

I guess that's when it happened. I don't know, but I started feeling...feeling better.

About myself. Life. *(Giggling.)* The weather...almost everything.

(She spins about.)

Nan, we need to brighten up this place. Why don't we get a new paint job. Maybe some slip covers. You know that really pretty embroidery, we could hang it over the couch.

(Jumping to another thought.) What about a vacation?!? You and I, we could go somewhere.

It wouldn't have to be expensive. You said Grandad and you did lots of little places upstate. I'm sure some still exit. It can't cost too much.

Oh, Nan. I'd like to go with you. You're...you're more than my grandmother. You're my friend. *(Stops. Looks at her grandmother and musters a bit of that special feeling.)* Nan, you are my very best friend.

Maybe some day, but right now I need to find me. If it's right, someday I'll find him or...he'll find me. Maybe he'll be like Grandad. Right now there's you and me. We take care of each other.

You are not a dottering old lady. Look at this place. I help but you...you're wonderful!

(Roz is again fluttering about the room.)

What about my job?

I'm entitled to a vacation. I haven't had one in...*(Realizing.)* It's almost four years. Then that was only a weekend.

(She spins again and then...)

Nan, I don't have to be a waitress.

It's okay. I can be a waitress if I want to, but I can also do anything I want. Anything.

You were right. You were always right. I should have listened. I could go back to school. So what if I quit! It doesn't matter how old I am. All I have to do is try...I could do something else.

I can't think of what or even if I want something else. I feel too good. Maybe I'll be Super Waitress. Maybe I'll just go to school and learn something. I wasted shool the last time. This time...this time I'll do better. Maybe even go to college. But, this time I'll try. I'll really try.

(Enthralled with her enlightenment.)

I can try, and try, and try again. I can do anything if I just...give myself the chance.

I know it all sounds crazy. But, wonderful-crazy. It has been a crazy-wonderful day. Ever since he came in.

(There is a moment of reflection.)

It's like when I was very little. I got hurt. You'd fix me. I'd cry. Then...I'd put my hand inside Grandad's; he'd pull me close and hug me.

I don't even remember him...what he looked like.

(Looking at her grandmother.) Mostly I remember you. He looked a lot like you. I remember us, and you were always there. *(Her happiness is undaunted but now filled with tears.)* Oh, Nan...Nan, I love you!

PART III

The following selections of monologues were created for special circumstances:

MASTECTOMY was written for an actress to audition at Producer level. She needed a specific speech that showed how a very vain woman dealt with the problems surrounding a mastectomy.

I developed LOVE BATTLE for a production company auditioning a specific type of actress as a general audition for a sexually oriented comedy. Each actress had two days to study the piece and present it. No information except the monologue was given to the performers.

EVENING OUT was used as a video spot, in 1971, to emphasize a No Smoking Campaign.

MY LOVER, THE HERO was from an early play that I have always felt needed to be rewritten. The monologue and one scene have survived. I used this monologue once, for general readings when I was directing a film for Great American Productions.

William-Alan Landes

Roslyn Witt

MASTECTOMY

EDNA. I look good -- don't I? Surprised? This outfit is really flattering.

I've always had nice looking legs. *(She turns slowly.)* Yes, my hips and waist are attractive. *(Slapping herself, both hands flat on her rump.)* A lot of men really like that. *(Thinking.)* It was difficult. I was always so vain. I guess I still am.

(Wandering.) I could never understand how the Renaissance men found it so flattering...all those paintings of women with stomachs. Round...fat tummys. *(She pats her stomach and smiles.)* Not mine. After the baby everybody said...but, they were wrong. I kept my shape. My shape! But now! *(Regaining her courage.)* Oh, well! *(She gathers a few pieces of clothes and finishes packing.)* It's really going to be difficult. John is not the supportive type...and everytime he looks at someone...I'm going to wonder. He's always been the jealous one...and I've loved it. Even if I never admitted it, I did keep him dangling. But now! I guess I'm jealous, too. I probably always have been...He is a very good looking man.

(Her glib air starts to deteriorate.)

We always were the best looking couple. I guess that was the most important...but now...*(Bravely.)* I don't think I'll look different...in clothing. What will it be like when we're alone?

I don't know if I can take any more of his sympathy! My mother and sister, they've been wonderful. Everybody's been so nice. I hate it!

Why does it have to be me? Why couldn't it be someone
else? There are so many ugly people.

My whole life has been centered around how I look
and...I won't even feel like a woman, now. Half a
woman. *(Reflecting.)* Half of something. I don't know
what...

I couldn't believe it! Just an ache; then a lump...I kept
lying to myself! When he said "There's no hope", I died.
I think I'd be better off if I did. I don't even have the
courage to die.

(Her emotions swell.) I don't want to be a freak! I'm a
woman and I want to be a whole woman -- but I can't...I
can't...*(She cries.)*

I couldn't even say the word. It took a week for me just to
mouth..."mastectomy..." *(Shouting.)* Mastectomy!

> *(There is a knock at the door. She quickly pulls
> herself together.)*

(Calling.) I'll only be a minute, Mom. I've got to get
something. *(She picks up her suitcase. Looks about the
room.)*

It's going to be strange...and looking in the mirror.
(She shakes her head "no" and exits.)

LOVE BATTLE

We've been married, 14 years. In all those years, I don't think I've ever been as content as I am now.

When we started dating...he was exciting. I was a small town girl and he...well, he just knew everything. He was always educating me; food, clothing, theatre, books, sex...SEX! Now, there's a subject!

Married fourteen years...daily if not more often for over eight years -- I don't think I...I...I never have...

It's nice to respect the man you marry. Jim's always had my respect. My love...God, I loved him. Over twice my age and I wanted him. A couple should be in love; to want him to hold you, to dream of his kisses; to need his passion. The passions should flow.

(Her sexual tone changes to boredom.) My evening's high point is hoping he'll fall asleep in front of the television.

Now, it's not all his fault. I was sixteen when we met. He was forty. I thought he had everything. *(Remembering.)* He did! I chased him. Even my parents were in favor of the marriage.

When I finished High School he took me on a cruise. Six months later I married him.

I don't regret the marriage. From poverty to riches in one easy step. What I do regret...I think I missed out...Love...I guess women dwell on the excitement of love. The most love I've had is in my fantasy or one of those Romance novels I've read. I long to be in love, to

Karen Flathers

worship a man; to need him passionately; to do anything he wants...anytime...*(Returning to reality.)* No, I've never really had a passionate experience. *(She sighs as she fights off new flights of fancy.)* Well, at least I can say I've been faithful. *(She giggles.)* Nobody's even asked! I wonder why? *(There is a moment as she contemplates her thoughts.)* I've been told I'm attractive. *(She looks at herself in the mirror.)* I am pretty! But, still...not once...not even a pass by one of Jim's friends.

There is the bright side of a blissful marriage, outside of money, *(Sarcastically)* those little things that make it all worthwhile. Our discussions...differences...*(Smiling.)* Arguments. I never thought it would be so much fun. *(Devilishly.)* It is! There is nothing better than a good argument.

It has reached the point where I find myself looking for things to be contrary about. If he's planning on fish for dinner...I'll make steak. He'll want me to wear my blue gown...I'll wear the peach. He's a Republican; I've taken a serious interest in the Democrats. I have gotten so good at it, if he says black I immediately think white.

(Excited.) I can cut his arguments to shreds. If I don't have a good case, then I just block him with my cold stare or shake my head. *(Bubbling.)* He can't stand it! Then if he raises his voice...I cry. That frustrates him. He doesn't know what to do. *(Reacting.)* I won't let him comfort me. I play hurt and obstinate. So when we go to bed...we go to sleep!

I may not have the lover's passion to delight the night - or anytime - but, there is great satisfaction in a good argument. I love it. The titilation of war of wits...the stimulation...the lust of words and...*(Smiling and touching herself.)* I always feel I look my best after a good fight. Ooh, how I love to fight!

Besides, he's fifty-nine. I'm only thirty-five. I may yet...(*Again, she laughs devilishly as she walks off.*)

EVENING OUT

(Entering. Looks around. Then, almost confidentially.) It happened last year. *(Correcting.)* No, actually thirteen months ago. *(Remembering.)* I'd gone to the theatre that night. Strange, the reason we change things and how it comes about. I never thought it would happen like that, but it did. *(Returning to the story.)* I didn't have a date. It was Friday. *(Smiling.)* I thought I was going to go out with...well, I didn't. Can't even remember why we didn't. Normally, I would have just stayed home. Instead, I got nicely dressed and took myself out. No intention of meeting or even looking for someone; just an indulgent evening...out on my own. I had a perfect dinner at this excellent Italian restaurant. Walking in the theatre district...I guess I was muttering or talking to myself..."Where should I eat?" This couple walking by answered me. "Marvelous Italian food. Two doors down from the corner. Very reasonable." They were gone. *(Looking up.)* Why not? So I went. *(Savoring the memory.)* Veal cutlet, lightly breaded in a wine sauce, vegetables...I can almost taste the hint of garlic, pasta, the cappuccino and pastry...Truely superb! *(Crosses left.)* I needed the walk back to the theatre. I ate too much. The walk helped. It was a show I had wanted to see for a long time, just never found the time. I was early so I stood in front of the theatre watching people. If I would have gone inside everything might have been different. *(Looking for something.)* I forgot my cigarettes! Maybe they'd have some inside...I could go up the block...why didn't I have a cigarette right after dinner? That was strange. I always smoked after a meal, usually with my coffee. But, I didn't that night! *(Turns.)* This man went by and it was like he was floating in a cloud of cigarette smoke. It seemed to engulf me. I'd been smoking since I was a teenager... *(Chidingly.)* Probably because my parents said I

couldn't...I went into the theatre and bought a pack. *(Crosses down.)* They only had those extra filtered things. Oh, well, I'll try them. While I was opening the pack I found myelf reading the Surgeon General's information..."Hazardous to your health"..."May cause cancer." "May cause fetal injury..." *(Realizing.)* I don't think I'd ever really paid any attention before. *(Critical.)* Smoking! I didn't really enjoy it! I usually couldn't even select a specific brand. *(Considering.)* It couldn't have been that health stuff? *(Brushing off the feeling. To audience.)* I quit smoking! *(Crossing up.)* Standing in front of the theatre I just quit. *(Stops. Turns to audience.)* There were a couple of times that I didn't think I was going to make it. But I did. Now, I don't even like to watch others smoke. I can't stand the smell. It's terrible to be with someone who smells like cigarettes. *(Starts off again. Stops.)* Maybe it was that health stuff. *(Thinks, shrugs her shoulders and walks off.)*

MY LOVER, THE HERO

This highly controversial one act play was originally performed by Theatre Unique during the summer of 1972. It was an extremely passionate depiction of an Ugly American, revealing two divergently different views of the same man. Korina gave up everything for her love, but Joe is not a villain.

Joe is a good American; served his country, during the war, and now as a statesman, not a politician. He never used Korina; he did not love her and he never said he did. They made love usually at her insistance. It was never his intention to hurt Korina, and when he discovered her pregnancy he wanted to help -- she wouldn't let him. Joe cares and still wants to help both Korina and their son.

Korina sees Joe through the distorted eyes of a woman hurt by her own love. Her depressing misinterpretation of the circumstances has overwhelmed everything she thinks, sees and does.

She is not a hateful or vengeful person. She loves her son and will always love Joe. If and when the circumstances were different, she accepted what they did as right and even necessary. Time, her love, and pain, have now blurred these actions. Her view of the facts surrounding their lives are also heavily burdened by a very different upbringing; she is not an American. But to her, her pain is very real.

In preparing this monologue the actress should emphasize Korina's view. She should de-emphasize and even ignore the textual information that Joe is really a good guy trapped in a one-sided love affair. The words Korina speaks should guide the performer on subtext, not ovewhelm the performance. If you are not careful, it is very easy for this cutting to deteriorate into a colorless outburst of a woman's unbridled scorn. To prevent this deterioration add more of the truthful information about Joe to the subtext.

Korina may use a foreign accent. It is not essential but if done well can add an interesting flavor to the performance.

(Korina has a standing picture frame in her hand and she speaks to it as if he were present.) You are a coward. A man without honor. *(She draws the picture to her breast and chokes on her words.)* My only friend. My greatest enemy. *(She draws a breath.)* My lover!

(She crosses right, still talking to the picture.) You have a small problem, so you come to me. You left me so little and again you come...to take more.

Ironic, but this time I think you are right to come. I can unload this anger, tell you about your shame and lessen the pain on my heart. You see, now and always I have and will love you. Maybe...maybe, you will suffer, just a little, to know what you have done.

I saved your life. *(Puts the picture down.)* It was on television...remember. You were a prisoner in my country. Hated! A spy! An Ugly American! I came to you, blinded by my love. When the generals wanted you shot. I pleaded your case. I begged my father to save you. He warned me not to love you. He was right!

You were spared and I was happy. We spent that summer together, in my country.

Then, you wanted some papers...information. You got what you wanted. My father died because I helped you. *(Remembering.)* He was a great man, my father. *(The memory evokes a tear.)* I betrayed him and my love, for you.

We escaped. The cost of lives...terrible...I can never go home!

I had you. I love you so! I thought I had your love. I knew I held your passion, but, I never knew you just used me.

Here in your country, you were a hero...the television...newspapers...Everyone idealized you. I...I too was a celebrity - a traitor who loved a man and betrayed her people, for him. I was a freak!

I thought it would pass and we could live quietly, together. But, it wasn't over. You needed more...more power...more fame...more... So again, you used me. I helped the one friend I had, in your country, to her destiny. She was a quiet girl, not too smart, scared, and we pushed her. You and I! I told her things...about her father...and her mother...about the old country...my country.

She killed him! She killed her father. We drove her crazy.

You took his place. You got...everything...everything you wanted. You became a leader, and you married his daughter...her sister!

Me with a child. A secret...a love I could not share. No home. No friends.

Now, you come again. I'm not fit, you say. Your wife cannot have a child. You want our son. You are a monster! I am a fool!

I love you yet, and your pain for my child tears me apart.

Here I am, and I consider -- Would the child of my love be better with his father and the woman who has him?

You do have everything. You offer to give everything to our son. But me...*(Her emotions building.)* again you offer nothing...nothing for me.

(Her emotions are mixed with tears, hurt and anger.) I only have a son's love -- you want to take it!

(Korina is overwhelmed by her emotions.) There should be a sign...a label...printed on each man. A sign, so a woman can see the true man from the false one. We have no understanding of men and we're blinded by love. I love you! *(She cries.)*

PART IV

The final selections are from new works.

A NEW COMPETITOR

This One Act Play has had several readings but has not been produced.

At the time of preparing this book A NEW COMPETITOR was being scheduled for a 1991 opening.

Susan Loomis, editor and chief of THE HERALD, has filled that gap of daughter and wife to her father, William Loomis, forty years Publisher of the town's leading newspaper. Susan has never wanted anything but to help her father but now there is something else. She has fiercely buried herself in a business and personal war with Roger Nelson, Publisher and Editor of a young newspaper THE RECORD.

Susan is out to destroy THE RECORD by destroying the owner, Mr. Nelson. But there is more, her attack is more personal than business. The title, we later discover, has a double entendre -- because the "New Competitor" is not Mr. Nelson or THE RECORD but Susan.

SUSAN. *(Enters. She is carrying a travel case in one hand and an attache in the other. She is older than her years...)* I'm back! Is that THE RECORD? *(She scans the newspaper.)* What has Continental Stores given them? *(Discovering the ad. Thunderstruck.)* A page! They only gave us a quarter page. We used to get a page for their Spring Sale. Then last year they gave us each a half page. Now, THE RECORD gets a page and we only get a quarter. The other advertisers may start to follow Continental's lead.

Roslyn Witt

It doesn't matter if we have two and a half pages more advertising.

We should be ahead! We've been publishing this paper for over forty years. In less than three years Nelson's RECORD has stolen our most profitable advertiser. At that rate by next year it will be us that has two and a half pages less than THE RECORD; then where will our forty years be?

(Her tone changes. She is uncomfortable. Embarrassed.) You know what I mean about "our forty years"...your years...but...I feel...we...

(Recovering her control. Struggling at first.) If we don't do something he's going to bankrupt us. That's why I visited Nancy Anderson in Clarkson.

I don't think it was a waste of time. Do you know who lived in Clarkson? *(Not waiting for a response.)* Our Mr. Nelson, owner of THE RECORD.

(Listening, then...) Could you have told me why he left Clarkson?

Do you really think Nelson would actually answer my questions? *(Answering her own question.)* Well, he wouldn't answer -- at least not with the truth. That's why I wasted my time and made the trip. We had to know!

(She produces the letter from her attache case.) Mrs. Anderson told me plenty and she gave me this. *(Opening the envelope, removes the letter and waves it at him.)* It's written to Mr. Anderson and signed Harvey Walker. *(Venomously.)* It was written by Roger Nelson and it is a forgery. Forgery!

Mr. Anderson spotted it and visited Mr. Nelson that afternoon. Nelson confessed everything. Mr. Anderson was a kind and gentle man, so he let Nelson quietly leave Clarkson without saying a word -- except to Mrs. Anderson. *(Smugly.)* That, Father, is the type of man we're dealing with -- WE HAVE HIM NOW!

STANDARDS

This monologue was cut from an evening of theatre titled
LADIES. It was based on an earlier production,
UNREASONABLE EXPECTATIONS (see PART I).
The show, a musical, consists of an all female cast and is
set in cosmopolitan America. To date LADIES has had
one reading for PLAYERS U.S.A. but has not been set for
production.

Janice Walker is a very attractive woman. She has
everything, *except a man.* She is very successful, with an
excellent business position, but would rather be a *non-
working* housewife. Janice has reached the age, whatever
that might be, where being with/having a man overwhlems
all other wants and desires.

Her view of life has taken shape, typically, as *the grass
is greener.* She feels that the time has come to enjoy life
and a woman can best serve herself by being at home,
supported by a man. Janice is definitely not the model for
women's equality.

Her standards in men are a reflection of how she sees
Mr. Perfect. Considering her track record, Janice has
always set her standards very high, maybe too high. She
has, for weeks, been trying to work up her courage to
discuss the problem with her mother.

Now, the subject open, she tells of what she wants in a
man. Mother clearly points out that daughter may be
unrealistic in her expectations and should stop trying to
create Mr. Perfection and start looking for Mr. Right.
Janice realizes that she is getting concerned about her
abilities to get a man and finally asks Mom for help.

Mom, I don't understand. It's always been that way.

I know. I'm pretty...but I just can't find him.

It just seems I'm always alone. I mean, I have friends but no one special. No one just for me. No one to love.

I love you too, Mom.

I don't care if I get married...just as long as he loves me and I love him.

My standards! I never thought they were too high. Maybe? *(She considers her mother's suggestion.)* No. My standards are just average. I want a man to love and love me.

He doesn't have to be special...well, maybe a little special...I want him to be handsome...He doesn't have to be tall...taller than me...even when I wear heels...but not too tall. I'm not looking for a muscle man but he needs to have a good build...what's real important is that he looks good when we get dressed up.

His hair? I don't care.

Well...I don't care what color. Blonde, brown, even black...I don't want him too old...gray! Men with gray hair always look old. I don't think I want a man that has gray hair.

Sports? What has that got to do with a man? I don't like watching sports. I don't want a man who watches the *game* all the time. Dad never watched games. I guess I want him to be like Dad.

Well, not like Dad. Dad was old. You're not old, Mom! I mean, Dad wasn't old for a father, but too old for me.

Money! I don't think that's important. *(Realizing.)* Well...it is, but...he doesn't have to be rich. *(Thinking.)* That doesn't mean he couldn't be rich; I wouldn't mind if he was. *(Supporting her position.)* I'd like him to have a good job...a good future...I wouldn't want him to be just *a worker.* Then we wouldn't have any money at all.

I don't want to work. I've been working since I got out of school. I think it's better if the man works and I stay home and take care of the house. *(Casually.)* I would want a maid. I don't like cleaning...and someone to do the laundry.

Shopping! I would do all the shopping.

Oh, not like the supermarket, the maid would do that. I'm better at shopping for clothing and the...important things. Besides, we could have lunch. I could meet my friends and do what I'm good at. *(Defensive.)* Oh, you know, Mom.

We'd have to have a nice house...in a good neighborhood! That would be very important.

I really don't think children are a good way to start out. I'd like to wait 'til I'm sure it works. You know how marriages...realtionships...they're so brittle these days.

I'm not hedging, Mom. I want to enjoy myself before I'm saddled with kids. There's so much I want and want from a man...I think it's more important to enjoy yourself before...

Mom! Okay, so I want a lot. *(Giving in.)* Maybe that's why I can't find anyone. Yes, I think I am. But, I hope I find someone before I compromise and start settling for *anyone.*

Sure I'll negotiate. My ideas are for Mr. Perfect but I'm not Miss Perfect. I'm Janice Walker...my cheerleader days are long gone...and all I really want is a man.

Mom, what am I doing wrong?

REGENCY TOWERS

This cutting was a last minute addition. It is taken from the first draft of a new work.

Michele could be almost any age, from a young girl to a mature woman. Her life has been filled with all that money could buy and overly devoted parents. She has not been oblivious to her personal aspects but just too busy indulging in the generosity of her life. A week ago, the bubble burst; she was confronted with the fact that she's unattractive, unpleasant, and overly self-indulgent. She tried to shrug it off but the reality permeated her entire being.

Michele finally took stock and discovered that she didn't like what she found. Being a strong-willed person, she vowed to make some changes. Knowing full well that if she was going to have any success, and very little physically could be done, she needed help...Jan's help; that's what friends are for. Michele does not see that Jan doesn't want to help, Jan likes things the way they are.

MICHELE: I have been thinking about this for some time. Finally, I've come to a conclusion. I want to tell you about it.

Stop that! I think you owe me the courtesy of listening. For a week you've been asking "What's wrong?"... "What's the matter?"..."Can't you talk to me?" Well, I'm ready to talk. Are you ready to listen?

Thank you.

I wouldn't have come here if you hadn't insisted. You called me. You asked me to come over.

Alright, so I wanted to talk. When you let something eat away at you and you think it all out, sometimes you just feel better if you can bounce your thoughts, conclusions, and ideas off another person.

You're always saying you're my friend...best friend. Maybe now is the time for you...

Alright, I'll ask. Please listen.

Mom and Dad have always given me everything. Well, everything a child really could have...Material things!

So I'm spoiled rotten. *(Laughs.)* It's true.

I was ten or eleven before I discovered that...well...You know how parents are. They always tell you how pretty you are and that the boys will love you and that you're cute...Well, I guess I believed them.

I know, they meant well; they always mean well. To them I really am pretty and cute and...their daughter. *(Coldly.)* But I'm not. *(She needs a moment to regain her composure.)*

I'm really not pretty or cute or...*(Bluntly.)* I'm a short, fat, rather dull looking person.

I know, I've got a great personality.

We both know what that's worth.

Jan, just listen. I don't need to be consoled. I've gone over it all. *(Bluntly.)* I'm not much in the looks department. I've seen the doctors; there's not much to

114

work with. And, as you joked, my personality is that of a spoiled brat. I'm abrasive.

If someone is going to marry me, he's going to get...a bitch...A real female dog.

Thank you. I don't see it. I'd like to, but I really don't think I'm going to change.

Yes. Right now, after a week of studying myself, I do feel I'll try to improve. And I will. Unforutnately, knowing me and at my age the final result will be a little better but not much.

I'm getting there. I do want to change. At least try. I'm going to work on it. Even a diet.

I don't expect much. *(Trying to bravely face her reality.)* If I'm lucky, there will be a little improvement in looks, a touch more on personality and with you as a watchdog...maybe...*(She pauses to regain composure.)* Maybe I can stop being a loser and...find someone...anyone. *(Slipping into tears; she inhales strongly to compose herself.)*

Please Jan, be my friend. Help me! I can't do it alone!

(She waits for an answer but Jan does not respond.) I don't want to be me. I don't...

SCENES for ACTING AND DIRECTING

PLAYING THE GAME

New Theatre Games

ABSURD BLACK AND COMIC SKETCHES

(Monologues and Duologues)

Fall 1992

SCENES for ACTING AND DIRECTING   vol. 2

SELECTIONS FROM SHAKESPEARE

(Monologues and Scenes)

Available from book stores or directly from:

· PLAYERS PRESS

P. O. Box 1132
Studio City, CA 91614-0132
U.S.A.

THE LIBRARY
WITHDRAWN
SWINDON